BLUES PLAY-ALONG

ok & CD for B♭, E♭, Bass Clef and C instruments

VOLUME 4

Shuffle BLUES

PLAY 8 SONGS WITH A PROFESSIONAL BAND

HOW TO USE THE CD:

Each song has <u>two</u> tracks:

1) Full Stereo Mix

All recorded instruments are present on this track.

2) Split Track

Piano and **Bass** parts can be removed
by turning down the volume on the LEFT channel.

Guitar parts can be removed
by turning down the volume on the RIGHT channel.

ISBN 978-1-4234-8669-5

HAL•LEONARD®
CORPORATION

7777 W. BLUEMOUND RD. P.O. BOX 13819 MILWAUKEE, WI 53213

Visit Hal Leonard Online at
www.halleonard.com

BOOK

CD

Beautician Blues

Words and Music by
B.B. King and Jules Bihari

VERSE
FREE TIME

1. I MET A FINE BEAU - TI - CIAN IN A

VER - Y FINE _____ CON - DI - TION. SHE WAS

MODERATELY ♩ = 132

LONG AND LEAN, AND YOU KNOW WHAT THAT MEANS. _ SHE'S A GOOD _ LOV-IN' MA-MA.

A HARD WORK-IN' WOM-AN. SHE MAKES _

_ A LOT OF MON-EY. I DON'T HAVE _ TO WOR - RY 'BOUT A THING.

VERSE

2. SHE WORKS HARD ALL DAY DRESS-IN' HAIR. _ MAN. _
3., 4. SEE ADDITIONAL LYRICS

YOU CAN BET I WAN-NA GET SOME - WHERE WITH MY GOOD LOV-IN' __ MA - MA,

MY HARD ___ WORK-IN' WOM-AN. SHE MAKES __

To Coda ⊕

___ A LOT OF MON-EY, I DON'T HAVE ___ TO WOR - RY 'BOUT A THING.

GUITAR SOLO

3. I MEET THE

D.S. al Coda

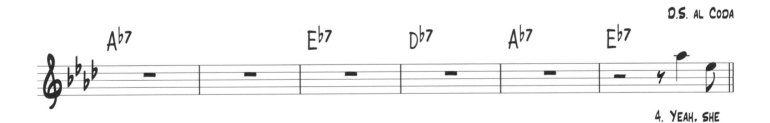

4. YEAH, SHE

⊕ CODA

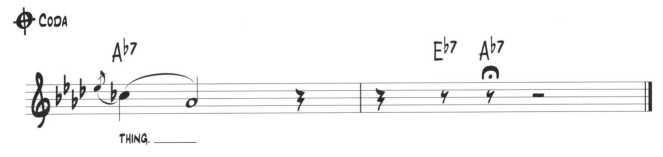

THING. ___

ADDITIONAL LYRICS

3. I MEET THE FINEST WOMEN FROM EV'RYWHERE,
BECAUSE MY BABY DRESS THEIR HAIR.
I'LL BE HER LOVER BOY, SHE TREATS ME LIKE A KING.
SHE MAKES A LOT OF MONEY,
DON'T HAVE TO WORRY 'BOUT A THING.

4. YEAH, SHE KEEPS HER HAIR SO NEAT AN' FINE,
AND EV'RY POUND OF HER IS MINE,
AND I'LL BE HER LOVER BOY, I'LL BE HAPPY AS A KING.
SHE MAKES A LOT OF MONEY,
DON'T HAVE TO WORRY 'BOUT A THING.

THE BLUES IS ALRIGHT

WORDS AND MUSIC BY
MILTON CAMPBELL

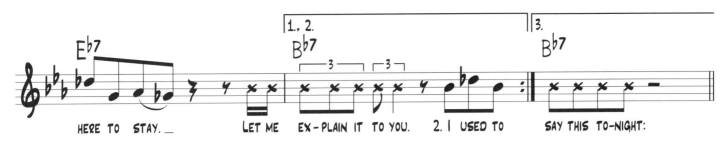

HERE TO STAY. ___   LET ME   EX-PLAIN IT TO YOU.   2. I USED TO   SAY THIS TO-NIGHT:

CHORUS

HEY,   HEY,   THE BLUES IS AL-RIGHT.   HEY,   HEY,   THE BLUES IS AL-RIGHT.   OH.

HEY,   HEY,   THE BLUES IS AL-RIGHT.   HEY,   HEY,   THE BLUES IS AL-RIGHT.   IT'S AL-

(ON D.S., FADE 3RD x)

RIGHT,   IT'S AL - RIGHT,   EV-'RY DAY AND   NIGHT.   LET'S TES-TI - FY, SOUND A-GAIN, Y'ALL.

I'M GON-NA   PLAY 'EM FOR YA   NOW.

I JUST GOT - TA SAY IT   AGAIN. YA'LL HELP ME.

DO   IT   A-GAIN.

GUITAR SOLO

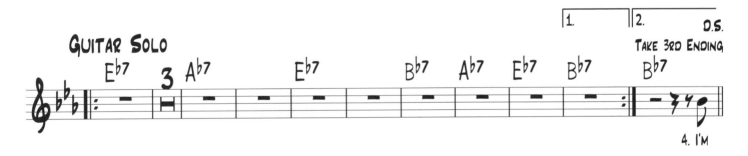

4. I'M

ADDITIONAL LYRICS

2. I USED TO HAVE SOMEONE THAT MEANT THE WHOLE WORLD TO ME.
BUT SHE LEFT ME FOR SOMEONE ELSE, LEFT MY HEART IN MISERY.
THAT'S WHEN I FOUND OUT THE BLUES WOULD ALWAYS BE A PART OF ME.
LET ME TELL YOU THIS:

3. YOU SEE, WHEN SHE LEFT ME, SHE GAVE ME THE BLUES, THAT WAS THE LAST THING I THOUGHT I COULD USE.
BUT NOW I'M GLAD SHE LEFT ME, I'M GLAD SHE GAVE ME THE BLUES.
YOU SEE, I WENT OUT AND FOUND ME, I WENT OUT AND FOUND ME SOMEONE NEW.
THAT'S WHY I CAN SAY THIS TONIGHT:

4. I'M GLAD SHE LEFT ME, I'M GLAD SHE GAVE ME THE BLUES.
YOU SEE, I'M GRATEFUL TO THE BLUES, IT WAS THE BLUES THAT BROUGHT ME TO YOU, YEAH.
YOU SEE, IF SHE HAD NEVER GIVEN ME THE BLUES, I NEVER WOULD HAVE FOUND SOMEONE SWEET LIKE YOU.
THAT'S WHY I CAN SAY, Y'ALL:

CD TRACK

③ Full Stereo Mix
⑪ Split Mix

C Version

Bright Lights, Big City

Words and Music by
Jimmy Reed

VERSE
MODERATELY ♩ = 92

1. Bright __ Lights, Big Cit - y, They

{ GOT / WENT } to my Ba - by's head. __ Oh, __ bright lights, a big

Cit - y, they { GOT / WENT } to my Ba - by's head. __ | __ Tried / | __ Hope

__ to tell the wom - an, but she don't be - lieve a word I said. __
__ you re - mem - ber a some of those things I said. __

VERSE

Fine (Fade last 2 bars)

__ 2. Go __ Light, Pret - ty Ba - by, __ A

NEED MY HELP SOME-DAY. ____ OH, ____ YES AL - RIGHT, A PRET-TY

BA - BY, ____ YOU'RE GON-NA NEED MY HELP _ SOME-DAY. ____ YOU'RE GON-NA

WISH YOU HAD A LIS-TENED TO SOME OF THOSE THINGS I SAID. ____

Solo

3. A GO ____

Verse

'HEAD _____ PRET-TY BA-BY, ___ A HON-EY, KNOCK A YOUR - SELF OUT. _

OH, ____ GO 'HEAD A PRET-TY BA - BY, ___ A

HON-EY, KNOCK _ YOUR - SELF OUT. ____ I ____ STILL ____ LOVE YOU BA - BY 'CAUSE YOU

D.S. al Fine

DON'T KNOW WHAT IT'S ALL A - BOUT. ____ 4. BRIGHT

9

Further on Up the Road

**Words and Music by
Joe Veasey and Don Robey**

BY, FUR-THER ON ___ UP THE ROAD. BA - BY,

MM, ___ YOU'LL ___ FIND OUT I WAS ___ RIGHT. ___

D.S. AL CODA

C7   F7   N.C.

4. FUR-THER ON ___ UP THE ROAD ___

⊕ CODA   F

NEW. ___

OUTRO   F7

MM, ___ BA -

Bb7

BY. FUR-THER ON ___ UP THE ROAD, ___ MM, ___

F7   C7

___ BA - BY. FUR - THER ON ___ UP THE ROAD, ___

Bb7   F7   F7#9 Eb9 E9 F9

MM, ___ YOU'LL GET YOURS. ___

Additional Lyrics

2. You got to reap just what you sow, that ol' saying is true. (x2)
Like you mistreat someone, someone's gonna mistreat you.

3. Now you're laughing, pretty baby, someday you're gonna be cryin'. (x2)
Further on up the road, you'll find out I wasn't lyin'.

4. Further on up the road, when you're all alone and blue. (x2)
You gonna ask me to take you back, baby, but I'll have somebody new.

I'M TORE DOWN

Words and Music by
Sonny Thompson

CD TRACK
5 Full Stereo Mix
13 Split Mix
C Version

Let Me Love You Baby

Words and Music by
Willie Dixon

ADDITIONAL LYRICS

2. Now, baby when you walk, you know you shake like a willow tree.
   Now, baby when you walk, you know you shake like a willow tree.
   A little girl like you would love to make a fool of me.

3. I'd give you all I own just for a little bit of your love.
   I'd give you all I own just for a little bit of your love.
   Since I met you baby, that's all I been livin' for.

Look At Little Sister

Words and Music by
Hank Ballard

VERSE

Moderately ♩ = 112

1. Hey, hey, hey, hey, hey, Ma-ma, look at lit-tle sis, out in the back-
2. See Verse 5 Lyrics

- yard shak-in' like this. Hey, hey, hey, hey, hey, hey,

Look at lit-tle sis - ter, hey. Hey, hey,

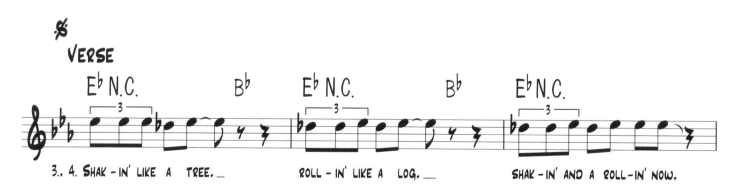

Hey, hey, Look at lit-tle sis - ter.

Verse

3., 4. Shak-in' like a tree, roll-in' like a log, shak-in' and a roll-in' now.

THAT AIN'T ALL. HEY, HEY, HEY, LOOK AT LIT-TLE SIS-

TER. HEY. HEY, HEY, HEY, HEY,

LOOK AT LIT-TLE SIS - TER.

SOLOS

D.S. AL CODA (2ND X)

CODA

VERSE

5. WHAT A-BOUT THE NEIGH - BORS, WHAT THEY GON-NA SAY?

STOP LIT-TLE SIS-TER, GET CAR-RIED A-WAY. HEY, HEY, HEY,

LOOK AT LIT-TLE SIS - TER. HEY. HEY, HEY,

HEY, HEY, OOH. LOOK AT LIT-TLE SIS - TER. OW!

Rock Me Baby

Words and Music by
B.B. King and Joe Bihari

Intro
Moderately ♩ = 90

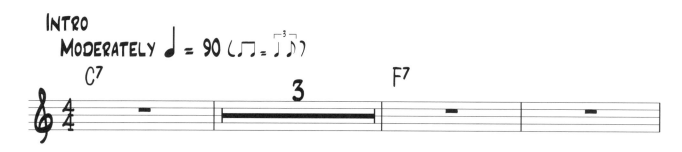

Verse

1. Rock me, ba - by,   Rock me all ___ night ___ long. ___

2., 3. See Additional Lyrics

Rock __ me, ba - by,   Hon - ey, rock me all ___ night long. _

I WANT YOU TO ROCK ME, BA - BY,

LIKE __ MY BACK __ AIN'T GOT NO BONE. __

GUITAR SOLO

ADDITIONAL LYRICS

2. ROLL ME, BABY, LIKE YOU ROLL A WAGON WHEEL.
   WANT YOU TO ROLL ME, BABY, LIKE YOU ROLL A WAGON WHEEL.
   WANT YOU TO ROLL ME, BABY, YOU DON'T KNOW HOW IT MAKE ME FEEL.

3. ROCK ME, BABY, HONEY, ROCK ME SLOW.
   HEY, ROCK ME, PRETTY BABY. BABY, ROCK ME SLOW.
   WANT YOU TO ROCK ME, BABY, 'TIL I WANT NO MORE.

Beautician Blues
Words and Music by
B.B. King and Jules Bihari

VERSE
FREE TIME

1. I MET A FINE BEAU - TI - CIAN IN A
VER - Y FINE CON - DI - TION. SHE WAS

MODERATELY ♩ = 132

LONG AND LEAN, AND YOU KNOW WHAT THAT MEANS. SHE'S A GOOD LOV - IN' MA - MA,
A HARD WORK - IN' WOM - AN. SHE MAKES
A LOT OF MON - EY. I DON'T HAVE TO WOR - RY 'BOUT A THING.

VERSE

2. SHE WORKS HARD ALL DAY DRESS - IN' HAIR. MAN.
3., 4. See Additional Lyrics

YOU CAN BET I WAN-NA GET SOME - WHERE WITH MY GOOD LOV - IN' ___ MA - MA,

MY HARD ___ WORK - IN' WOM - AN. SHE MAKES __

___ A LOT OF MON-EY, I DON'T HAVE __ TO WOR - RY 'BOUT A THING.

GUITAR SOLO

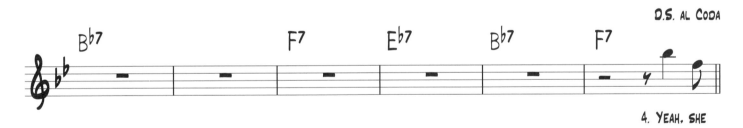

3. I MEET THE

D.S. AL CODA

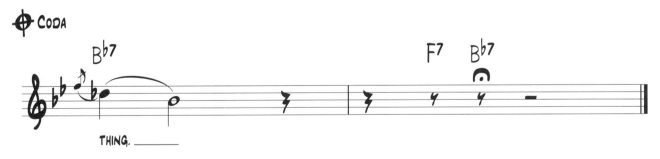

4. YEAH, SHE

THING. ___

ADDITIONAL LYRICS

3. I MEET THE FINEST WOMEN FROM EV'RYWHERE,
BECAUSE MY BABY DRESS THEIR HAIR.
I'LL BE HER LOVER BOY, SHE TREATS ME LIKE A KING.
SHE MAKES A LOT OF MONEY,
DON'T HAVE TO WORRY 'BOUT A THING.

4. YEAH, SHE KEEPS HER HAIR SO NEAT AN' FINE,
AND EV'RY POUND OF HER IS MINE,
AND I'LL BE HER LOVER BOY, I'LL BE HAPPY AS A KING.
SHE MAKES A LOT OF MONEY,
DON'T HAVE TO WORRY 'BOUT A THING.

The Blues Is Alright
Words and Music by
Milton Campbell

Additional Lyrics

2. I used to have someone that meant the whole world to me.
   But she left me for someone else, left my heart in misery.
   That's when I found out the blues would always be a part of me.
   Let me tell you this:

3. You see, when she left me, she gave me the blues, that was the last thing I thought I could use.
   But now I'm glad she left me, I'm glad she gave me the blues.
   You see, I went out and found me, I went out and found me someone new.
   That's why I can say this tonight:

4. I'm glad she left me, I'm glad she gave me the blues.
   You see, I'm grateful to the blues, it was the blues that brought me to you, yeah.
   You see, if she had never given me the blues, I never would have found someone sweet like you.
   That's why I can say, y'all:

Bright Lights, Big City

Words and Music by
Jimmy Reed

VERSE
Moderately ♩ = 92

1. Bright ___ lights, big cit - y, they

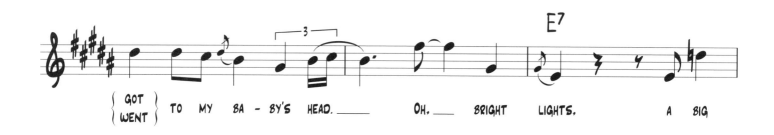

{ GOT / WENT } to my ba - by's head. ___ Oh, ___ bright lights, a big

cit - y, they { GOT / WENT } to my ba - by's head. ___ { I ___ tried / I ___ hope }

___ to tell the wom - an, but she don't be - lieve a word I said. ___
___ you re - mem - ber a some of those things I said. ___

VERSE

Fine (Fade last 2 bars)

___ 2. Go ___ light, pret - ty ba - by, ___ A

NEED MY HELP SOME-DAY. ___ OH, ___ YES AL - RIGHT, A PRET-TY

BA - BY, ___ YOU'RE GON-NA NEED MY HELP ___ SOME-DAY. ___ YOU'RE GON-NA

WISH YOU HAD A LIS-TENED TO SOME OF THOSE THINGS I SAID. ___

SOLO

3. A GO ___

VERSE

'HEAD ___ PRET-TY BA - BY, ___ A HON-EY, KNOCK A YOUR - SELF OUT. ___

OH, ___ GO 'HEAD A PRET - TY BA - BY, ___ A

HON-EY, KNOCK ___ YOUR - SELF OUT. ___ I ___ STILL ___ LOVE YOU BA - BY 'CAUSE YOU

D.S. al Fine

DON'T KNOW WHAT IT'S ALL A - BOUT. ___ 4. BRIGHT

Additional Lyrics

2. You got to reap just what you sow, that ol' saying is true. (x2)
   Like you mistreat someone, someone's gonna mistreat you.

3. Now you're laughing, pretty baby, someday you're gonna be cryin'. (x2)
   Further on up the road, you'll find out I wasn't lyin'.

4. Further on up the road, when you're all alone and blue, (x2)
   You gonna ask me to take you back, baby, but I'll have somebody new.

I FEEL LIKE THIS WHEN MY BA-BY CAN'T BE FOUND? __

VERSE

2. I LOVE YOU, BA-BY, WITH ALL MY HEART AND SOUL. A
LOVE YOU, BA-BY, WITH ALL MY MIGHTS. A

LOVE LIKE MINE __ WILL __ NEV-ER GROW OLD. I LOVE YOU IN THE MORN-ING AND IN THE
LOVE LIKE MINE __ IS OUT-TA SIGHT. I'LL DIE FOR YOU __ IF YOU

EVE - NIN' TOO. __ BUT EV - 'RY TIME YOU LEAVE ME, I GET MAD WITH YOU. } WELL, I'M
WANT ME TO. __ I REAL-LY DON'T BE-LIEVE YOUR LOVE IS TRUE. }

CHORUS

TORE DOWN. I'M AL - MOST LEV-EL WITH THE GROUND. To Coda 1

WHY D' I FEEL LIKE __ THIS __ WHEN MY BA-BY CAN'T BE FOUND? __

GUITAR SOLO

D.S. AL CODA 1

3.1

Coda 1   D.S.S. AL CODA 2   Coda 2

A WELL, I'M   MY BA-BY CAN'T BE FOUND? __

CD TRACK
6 Full Stereo Mix
14 Split Mix

Bb Version

Let Me Love You Baby

Words and Music by
Willie Dixon

2., 3. See Additional Lyrics

YES, LET ___ ME LOVE ___ YOU, BABE. _____ LET ME

LOVE YOU, BA - BY, 'TIL YOUR GOOD_ LOVE_ DRIVE _____ ME CRA - ZY.

To Coda ⊕

GUITAR SOLO

YEAH. (1ST X ONLY) YEAH. I AIN'T LY - IN'.

YOU ARE. HELP ME OUT, WOM - AN.

D.S. al CODA
TAKE 2ND ENDING

YEAH. 3. I'LL ___ GIVE YOU

⊕ CODA   GUITAR SOLO

REPEAT & FADE 3RD X

ADDITIONAL LYRICS

2. NOW, BABY WHEN YOU WALK, YOU KNOW YOU SHAKE LIKE A WILLOW TREE.
   NOW, BABY WHEN YOU WALK, YOU KNOW YOU SHAKE LIKE A WILLOW TREE.
   A LITTLE GIRL LIKE YOU WOULD LOVE TO MAKE A FOOL OF ME.

3. I'D GIVE YOU ALL I OWN JUST FOR A LITTLE BIT OF YOUR LOVE.
   I'D GIVE YOU ALL I OWN JUST FOR A LITTLE BIT OF YOUR LOVE.
   SINCE I MET YOU BABY, THAT'S ALL I BEEN LIVIN' FOR.

B♭ Version

Look At Little Sister

Words and Music by
Hank Ballard

VERSE

Moderately ♩ = 112

1. Hey, hey, hey, hey, hey, Ma-ma, look at lit-tle sis, out in the back-
2. See Verse 5 Lyrics

- yard shak-in' like ___ this. ___ Hey, hey, hey, hey, hey, hey,

Look at lit-tle sis - ter, hey. ___ Hey, hey,

Hey, hey, ___ Look at lit-tle sis - ter.

VERSE

3., 4. Shak-in' like a tree. ___ Roll-in' like a log. ___ Shak-in' and a roll-in' now.

Bb Version

Rock Me Baby

Words and Music by
B.B. King and Joe Bihari

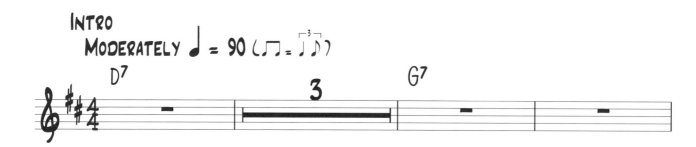

INTRO
MODERATELY ♩ = 90

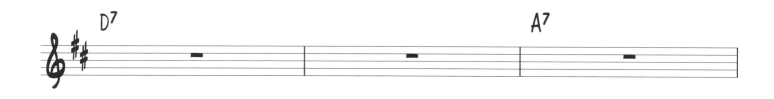

VERSE

1. Rock me, ba - by,   Rock me all __ night   long.
2., 3. See Additional Lyrics

Rock __ me, ba - by,   hon - ey, rock me all ___ night long. __

I WANT YOU TO ROCK ME, BA - BY,

LIKE ___ MY BACK ___ AIN'T GOT NO BONE. ___

GUITAR SOLO

CODA

FADE OUT

ADDITIONAL LYRICS

2. ROLL ME, BABY, LIKE YOU ROLL A WAGON WHEEL.
   WANT YOU TO ROLL ME, BABY, LIKE YOU ROLL A WAGON WHEEL.
   WANT YOU TO ROLL ME, BABY, YOU DON'T KNOW HOW IT MAKE ME FEEL.

3. ROCK ME, BABY, HONEY, ROCK ME SLOW.
   HEY, ROCK ME, PRETTY BABY. BABY, ROCK ME SLOW.
   WANT YOU TO ROCK ME, BABY, 'TIL I WANT NO MORE.

Beautician Blues

Words and Music by
B.B. King and Jules Bihari

VERSE
Free Time

1. I met a fine beau-ti-cian in a ver-y fine con-di-tion. She was

Moderately ♩ = 132

long and lean, and you know what that means. She's a good lov-in' ma-ma, a hard work-in' wom-an. She makes a lot of mon-ey, I don't have to wor-ry 'bout a thing.

VERSE

2. She works hard all day dress-in' hair. Man,
3., 4. See Additional Lyrics

YOU CAN BET I WAN-NA GET SOME-WHERE_ WITH MY GOOD LOV-IN'_ MA-MA.

MY HARD ____ WORK-IN' WOM-AN. SHE MAKES _

____ A LOT OF MON-EY, I DON'T HAVE __ TO WOR - RY 'BOUT A THING.

Guitar Solo

3. I MEET THE

4. YEAH, SHE

THING. _____

Additional Lyrics

3. I MEET THE FINEST WOMEN FROM EV'RYWHERE,
BECAUSE MY BABY DRESS THEIR HAIR.
I'LL BE HER LOVER BOY, SHE TREATS ME LIKE A KING.
SHE MAKES A LOT OF MONEY,
DON'T HAVE TO WORRY 'BOUT A THING.

4. YEAH, SHE KEEPS HER HAIR SO NEAT AN' FINE,
AND EV'RY POUND OF HER IS MINE,
AND I'LL BE HER LOVER BOY, I'LL BE HAPPY AS A KING.
SHE MAKES A LOT OF MONEY,
DON'T HAVE TO WORRY 'BOUT A THING.

CD TRACK

2 FULL STEREO MIX

10 SPLIT MIX

Eb VERSION

The Blues Is Alright

WORDS AND MUSIC BY
MILTON CAMPBELL

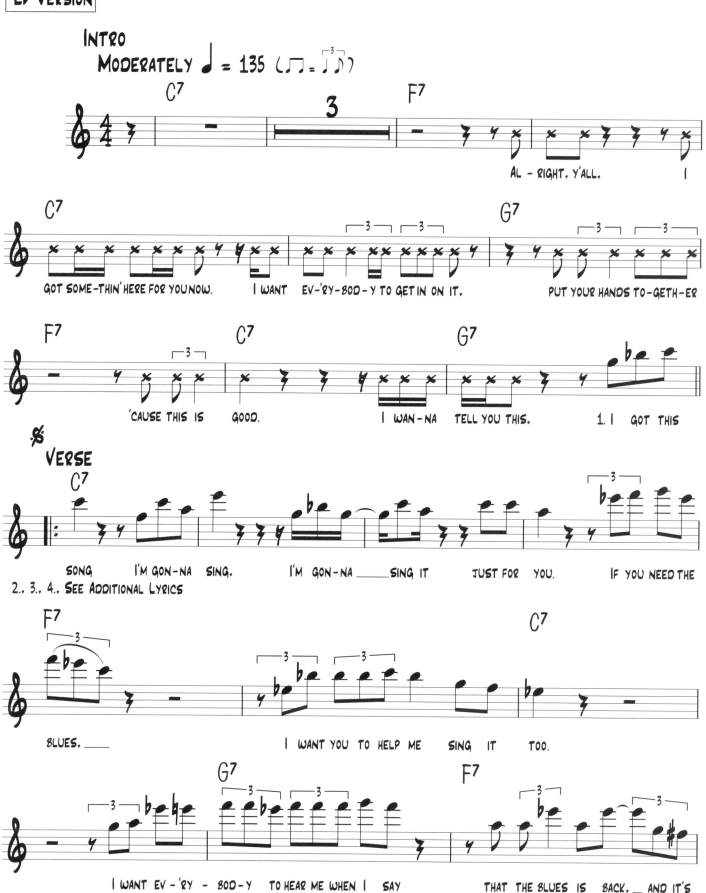

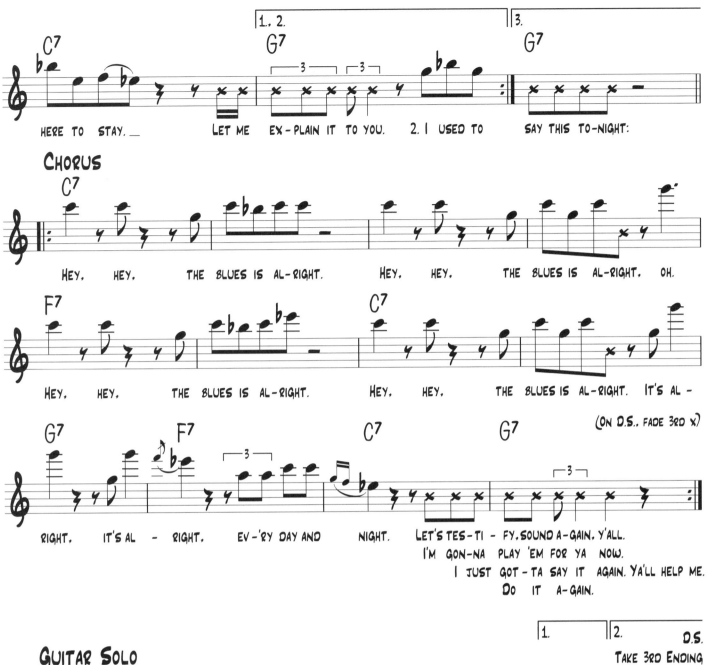

HERE TO STAY. ___   LET ME EX-PLAIN IT TO YOU.   2. I USED TO   SAY THIS TO-NIGHT:

Chorus

HEY, HEY, THE BLUES IS AL-RIGHT.   HEY, HEY, THE BLUES IS AL-RIGHT. OH.

HEY, HEY, THE BLUES IS AL-RIGHT.   HEY, HEY, THE BLUES IS AL-RIGHT. IT'S AL-

(ON D.S., FADE 3RD X)

RIGHT. IT'S AL - RIGHT. EV-'RY DAY AND NIGHT.

LET'S TES-TI - FY, SOUND A-GAIN, Y'ALL.
I'M GON-NA PLAY 'EM FOR YA NOW.
I JUST GOT-TA SAY IT AGAIN. YA'LL HELP ME.
DO IT A-GAIN.

Guitar Solo

D.S.
TAKE 3RD ENDING

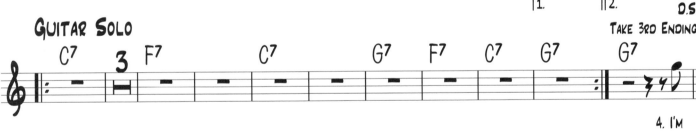

4. I'M

Additional Lyrics

2. I USED TO HAVE SOMEONE THAT MEANT THE WHOLE WORLD TO ME.
BUT SHE LEFT ME FOR SOMEONE ELSE, LEFT MY HEART IN MISERY.
THAT'S WHEN I FOUND OUT THE BLUES WOULD ALWAYS BE A PART OF ME.
LET ME TELL YOU THIS:

3. YOU SEE, WHEN SHE LEFT ME, SHE GAVE ME THE BLUES, THAT WAS THE LAST THING I THOUGHT I COULD USE.
BUT NOW I'M GLAD SHE LEFT ME, I'M GLAD SHE GAVE ME THE BLUES.
YOU SEE, I WENT OUT AND FOUND ME, I WENT OUT AND FOUND ME SOMEONE NEW.
THAT'S WHY I CAN SAY THIS TONIGHT:

4. I'M GLAD SHE LEFT ME, I'M GLAD SHE GAVE ME THE BLUES.
YOU SEE, I'M GRATEFUL TO THE BLUES, IT WAS THE BLUES THAT BROUGHT ME TO YOU, YEAH.
YOU SEE, IF SHE HAD NEVER GIVEN ME THE BLUES, I NEVER WOULD HAVE FOUND SOMEONE SWEET LIKE YOU.
THAT'S WHY I CAN SAY, Y'ALL:

Bright Lights, Big City
Words and Music by
Jimmy Reed

VERSE
Moderately ♩ = 92 (♫ = ♪♪)

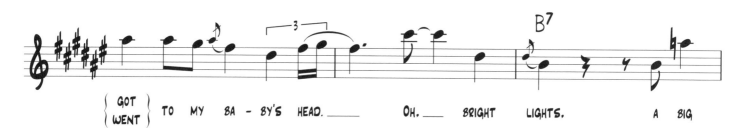

1. Bright ___ lights, big cit-y, they

{GOT / WENT} to my ba-by's head. ___ Oh, ___ bright lights, a big

cit-y, they {GOT / WENT} to my ba-by's head. ___

I ___ tried ___
I ___ hope ___

___ to tell the wom-an, but she don't be-lieve a word I said. ___
___ you re-mem-ber a some of those things I said. ___

VERSE
Fine (Fade last 2 bars)

___
2. Go ___ light, pret-ty ba-by, ___ A

NEED MY HELP SOME-DAY. ___ OH, ___ YES AL - RIGHT, A PRET-TY

BA - BY, ___ YOU'RE GON-NA NEED MY HELP _ SOME-DAY. ___ YOU'RE GON-NA

WISH YOU HAD A LIS-TENED TO SOME OF THOSE THINGS I SAID. ___

SOLO

3

3. A GO ___

VERSE

'HEAD ___ PRET-TY BA-BY, ___ A HON-EY, KNOCK A YOUR - SELF OUT. ___

___ OH, ___ GO 'HEAD A PRET-TY BA-BY, ___ A

HON-EY, KNOCK _ YOUR - SELF OUT. ___ I ___ STILL ___ LOVE YOU BA-BY 'CAUSE YOU

D.S. AL FINE

DON'T KNOW WHAT IT'S ALL A - BOUT. ___ 4. BRIGHT

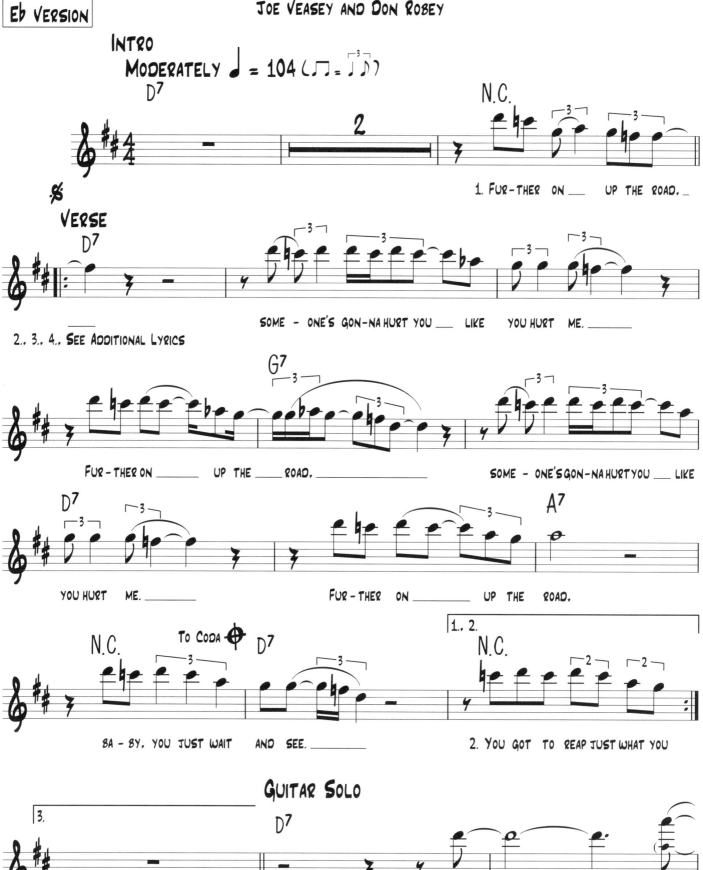

Further On Up the Road

Words and Music by
Joe Veasey and Don Robey

Guitar Solo

BY,   FUR-THER ON ___ UP THE ROAD, BA - BY,

MM, ___ YOU'LL ___ FIND OUT I WAS ___ RIGHT. ___

N.C.   D.S. AL CODA

4. FUR-THER ON ___ UP THE ROAD ___

Coda

NEW. ___

Outro

MM. ___ BA -

BY,   FUR-THER   ON ___ UP THE ROAD. ___ MM. ___

BA - BY.   FUR - THER ON ___ UP THE ROAD, _

MM. ___ YOU'LL _ GET   YOURS. ___

Additional Lyrics

2. YOU GOT TO REAP JUST WHAT YOU SOW, THAT OL' SAYING IS TRUE. (x2)
   LIKE YOU MISTREAT SOMEONE, SOMEONE'S GONNA MISTREAT YOU.

3. NOW YOU'RE LAUGHING, PRETTY BABY, SOMEDAY YOU'RE GONNA BE CRYIN'. (x2)
   FURTHER ON UP THE ROAD, YOU'LL FIND OUT I WASN'T LYIN'.

4. FURTHER ON UP THE ROAD, WHEN YOU'RE ALL ALONE AND BLUE. (x2)
   YOU GONNA ASK ME TO TAKE YOU BACK, BABY, BUT I'LL HAVE SOMEBODY NEW.

I'm Tore Down

Words and Music by
Sonny Thompson

I FEEL LIKE THIS WHEN MY BA-BY CAN'T BE FOUND?

%. VERSE

2. I LOVE YOU, BA-BY, WITH ALL MY HEART AND SOUL. A
I LOVE YOU, BA-BY, WITH ALL MY MIGHTS. A

LOVE LIKE MINE WILL NEV-ER GROW OLD. I LOVE YOU IN THE MORN-ING AND IN THE
LOVE LIKE MINE IS OUT-TA SIGHT. I'LL DIE FOR YOU IF YOU

EVE-NIN' TOO. BUT EV-'RY TIME YOU LEAVE ME, I GET MAD WITH YOU. } WELL, I'M
WANT ME TO. I REAL-LY DON'T BE-LIEVE YOUR LOVE IS TRUE. }

CHORUS

TORE DOWN. I'M AL-MOST LEV-EL WITH THE GROUND.

To Coda 1

WHY D' I FEEL LIKE THIS WHEN MY BA-BY CAN'T BE FOUND?

GUITAR SOLO

D.S. al Coda 1

3. I

Coda 1 D.S.S. al Coda 2 Coda 2

A WELL, I'M MY BA-BY CAN'T BE FOUND?

45

Let Me Love You Baby

Words and Music by
Willie Dixon

Look At Little Sister

Words and Music by
Hank Ballard

VERSE

1. Hey, hey, hey, hey, hey, Ma-ma, look at lit-tle sis, out in the back-
2. See Verse 5 Lyrics

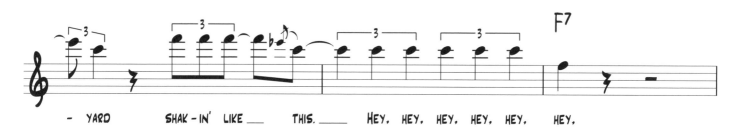

- yard shak-in' like this. Hey, hey, hey, hey, hey, hey,

look at lit-tle sis - ter, hey. Hey, hey,

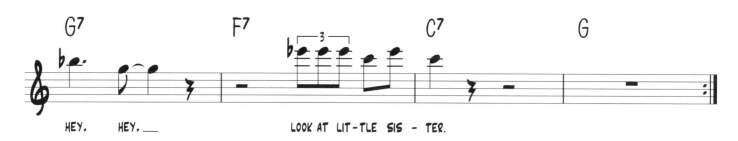

Hey, hey, look at lit-tle sis - ter.

VERSE

3., 4. Shak-in' like a tree. roll-in' like a log, shak-in' and a roll-in' now.

48

Rock Me Baby

Words and Music by
B.B. King and Joe Bihari

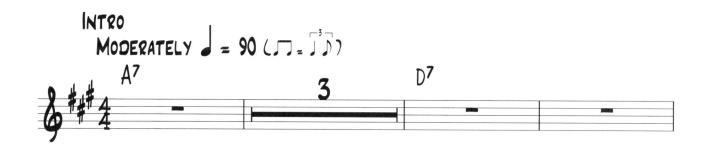

1. Rock me, ba - by, Rock me all ___ night long. ___

2., 3. See Additional Lyrics

Rock ___ me, ba - by, Hon - ey, rock me all ___ night long. ___

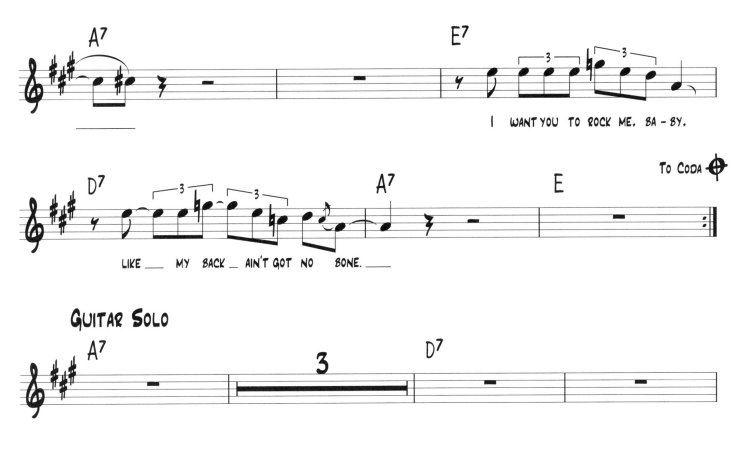

I WANT YOU TO ROCK ME, BA-BY,

LIKE ___ MY BACK ___ AIN'T GOT NO BONE. ___

GUITAR SOLO

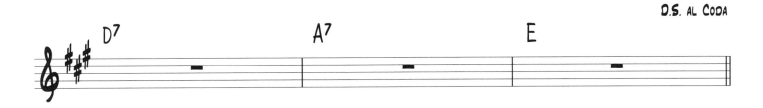

CODA

ADDITIONAL LYRICS

2. ROLL ME, BABY, LIKE YOU ROLL A WAGON WHEEL.
   WANT YOU TO ROLL ME, BABY, LIKE YOU ROLL A WAGON WHEEL.
   WANT YOU TO ROLL ME, BABY, YOU DON'T KNOW HOW IT MAKE ME FEEL.

3. ROCK ME, BABY, HONEY, ROCK ME SLOW.
   HEY, ROCK ME, PRETTY BABY. BABY, ROCK ME SLOW.
   WANT YOU TO ROCK ME, BABY, 'TIL I WANT NO MORE.

𝄢 C Version

Beautician Blues
Words and Music by
B.B. King and Jules Bihari

VERSE
FREE TIME

Moderately ♩ = 132

2. She works hard all day dress-in' hair.___ Man,___
3., 4. See Additional Lyrics

YOU CAN BET I WAN-NA GET SOME - WHERE_ WITH MY GOOD LOV-IN'_ MA - MA,

MY HARD _____ WORK - IN' WOM - AN. SHE MAKES _

A LOT OF MON-EY, I DON'T HAVE _ TO WOR - RY 'BOUT A THING.

GUITAR SOLO

3. I MEET THE

D.S. AL CODA

4. YEAH, SHE

⊕ CODA

THING. _____

ADDITIONAL LYRICS

3. I MEET THE FINEST WOMEN FROM EV'RYWHERE,
BECAUSE MY BABY DRESS THEIR HAIR.
I'LL BE HER LOVER BOY, SHE TREATS ME LIKE A KING.
SHE MAKES A LOT OF MONEY,
DON'T HAVE TO WORRY 'BOUT A THING.

4. YEAH, SHE KEEPS HER HAIR SO NEAT AN' FINE,
AND EV'RY POUND OF HER IS MINE.
AND I'LL BE HER LOVER BOY, I'LL BE HAPPY AS A KING.
SHE MAKES A LOT OF MONEY,
DON'T HAVE TO WORRY 'BOUT A THING.

The Blues Is Alright
Words and Music by
Milton Campbell

ADDITIONAL LYRICS

2. I used to have someone that meant the whole world to me.
   But she left me for someone else, left my heart in misery.
   That's when I found out the blues would always be a part of me.
   Let me tell you this:

3. You see, when she left me, she gave me the blues, that was the last thing I thought I could use.
   But now I'm glad she left me, I'm glad she gave me the blues.
   You see, I went out and found me, I went out and found me someone new.
   That's why I can say this tonight:

4. I'm glad she left me, I'm glad she gave me the blues.
   You see, I'm grateful to the blues, it was the blues that brought me to you, yeah.
   You see, if she had never given me the blues, I never would have found someone sweet like you.
   That's why I can say, y'all:

CD TRACK

③ Full Stereo Mix
⑪ Split Mix

𝄢 C Version

Bright Lights, Big City

Words and Music by
Jimmy Reed

VERSE
Moderately ♩ = 92

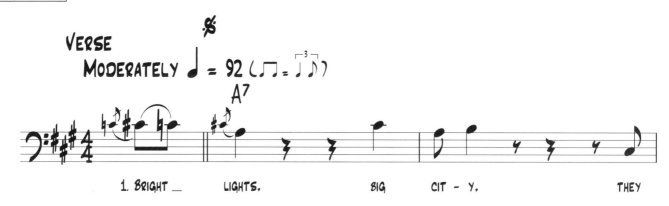

A⁷

1. Bright ___ lights, big cit - y, they

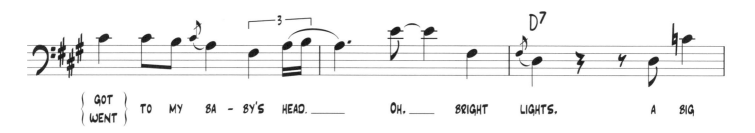

D⁷

{ GOT } to my ba - by's head. ___ Oh, ___ bright lights, a big
{ WENT }

A⁷

cit - y, they { GOT } to my ba - by's head. ___ { I ___ TRIED }
               { WENT }   { I ___ HOPE ___ }

E⁷   D⁷

___ to tell the wom - an, but she don't be - lieve a word I said. ___
___ you re - mem - ber a some of those things I said. ___

VERSE
Fine (Fade last 2 bars)

A⁷   E⁷   A⁷

___ }   2. Go ___ light, pret - ty ba - by, ___ A

FURTHER ON UP THE ROAD

Words and Music by
Joe Veasey and Don Robey

Additional Lyrics

2. You got to reap just what you sow, that ol' saying is true. (x2)
   Like you mistreat someone, someone's gonna mistreat you.

3. Now you're laughing, pretty baby, someday you're gonna be cryin'. (x2)
   Further on up the road, you'll find out I wasn't lyin'.

4. Further on up the road, when you're all alone and blue. (x2)
   You gonna ask me to take you back, baby, but I'll have somebody new.

I'm Tore Down

Words and Music by
Sonny Thompson

LET ME LOVE YOU BABY

WORDS AND MUSIC BY
WILLIE DIXON

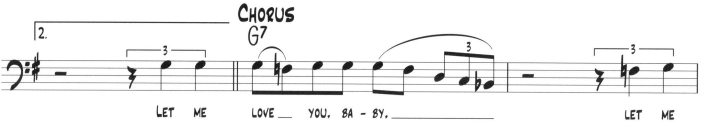

Look At Little Sister

Words and Music by
Hank Ballard

Verse

Moderately ♩ = 112

1. Hey, hey, hey, hey, hey, Ma-ma, look at lit-tle sis, out in the back-
2. See Verse 5 Lyrics

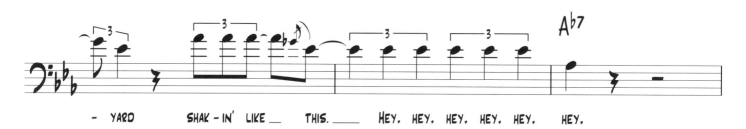

- yard shak-in' like __ this. __ Hey, hey, hey, hey, hey, hey.

Look at lit-tle sis - ter, hey. _____ Hey, hey.

Hey, hey, __ Look at lit-tle sis - ter.

Verse

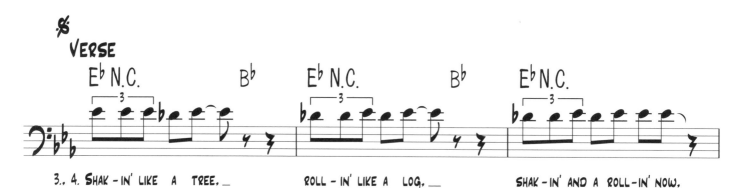

3., 4. Shak-in' like a tree. __ Roll-in' like a log. __ Shak-in' and a roll-in' now.

THAT AIN'T ALL.___ HEY, HEY,   HEY,   LOOK AT LIT-TLE SIS-

TER.   HEY. _____   HEY, HEY,   HEY,   HEY, ___

LOOK AT LIT-TLE SIS - TER.

5. WHAT A-BOUT THE NEIGH - BORS,   WHAT THEY GON-NA SAY?___

STOP LIT-TLE SIS-TER, GET   CAR - RIED A-WAY.___ HEY, HEY,   HEY,

LOOK AT LIT-TLE SIS - TER.   HEY. _____   HEY, HEY,

HEY, HEY,___   OOH.___   LOOK AT LIT-TLE SIS - TER.   OW!

65

9: C Version

Rock Me Baby

Words and Music by
B.B. King and Joe Bihari

INTRO
MODERATELY ♩ = 90

C7   F7

C7   G7

F7   C7   G

% VERSE
C7

1. Rock me, ba - by,   Rock me all ___ night long. ___
2., 3. See Additional Lyrics

F7

Rock __ me, ba - by,   Hon - ey, rock me all ___ night long.

66

I WANT YOU TO ROCK ME, BA - BY.

LIKE ___ MY BACK ___ AIN'T GOT NO ___ BONE. ___

GUITAR SOLO

Additional Lyrics

2. Roll me, baby, like you roll a wagon wheel.
   Want you to roll me, baby, like you roll a wagon wheel.
   Want you to roll me, baby, you don't know how it make me feel.

3. Rock me, baby, honey, rock me slow.
   Hey, rock me, pretty baby. Baby, rock me slow.
   Want you to rock me, baby, 'til I want no more.

Presenting the Hal Leonard JAZZ PLAY-ALONG® SERIES

For use with all B-flat, E-flat, Bass Clef and C instruments, the Jazz Play-Along® Series is the ultimate learning tool for all jazz musicians. With musician-friendly lead sheets, melody cues, and other split-track choices on the included CD, these first-of-a-kind packages help you master improvisation while playing some of the greatest tunes of all time. FOR STUDY, each tune includes a split track with: melody cue with proper style and inflection • professional rhythm tracks • choruses for soloing • removable bass part • removable piano part. FOR PERFORMANCE, each tune also has: an additional full stereo accompaniment track (no melody) • additional choruses for soloing.

0910

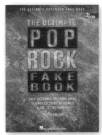
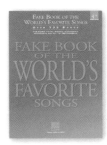